What We Do in Lent

A Child's Activity Book

Anne E. Kitch

Illustrations by Dorothy Thompson Perez

MOREHOUSE PUBLISHING

HARRISBURG · NEW YORK

Morehouse Publishing, 4775 Linglestown Road, Harrisburg, PA 17105

Morehouse Publishing, 445 Fifth Avenue, New York, NY 10016

Morehouse Publishing is an imprint of Church Publishing Incorporated.

Cover art by Dorothy Thompson Perez

Cover design by Corey Kent

Printed in the United States of America

07 08 09 10 11 12 10 9 8 7 6 5 4 3 2 1

ISBN 978-0-8192-2278-7

The Forty Days of Lent: The Fast before the Feast

Lent is the season before Easter. Because Easter is a great feast of the Church, we prepare for it by a season of penitence. We fast before we feast. Lent lasts forty days, beginning on Ash Wednesday and continuing through Holy Week. Sundays are not included in these forty days, because every Sunday is a feast of the resurrection. Thus, Sundays are never fast days. That's why we call them the Sundays *in* Lent, not the Sundays *of* Lent. Ash Wednesday and the weekdays of Lent are days of special devotion and self-denial.

In the early days of the Church, this fast before Easter lasted only two or three days. The focus of this time was placed on the candidates preparing for baptism at the Great Vigil of Easter. But as the theology of the Church Year developed, this time of fasting was extended to forty days to recall the forty days that Jesus spent fasting in the wilderness. Observing the fast of Lent became part of the spiritual discipline of the entire Church.

Fasting is considered a spiritual discipline because it helps us pay more attention. When we fast, we suddenly notice food and how much it occupies our lives. By recognizing this, we can redirect some of our energy that is spent on the pleasure of food toward other important matters. When fasting is described in scripture, it is almost always accompanied by prayer. Traditionally, certain foods are omitted on fast days, such as meat, eggs, butter, and cheese. The celebration of Shrove (or Fat) Tuesday originated as a day to clean out the cupboard of all these forbidden foods before the great fast of Lent began.

But our Lenten fast does not need to be only about food. We can also fast from other things, such as behaviors, which draw our attention away from God. Fasting in this way can help us to become more aware of those who are not as "full" as we are. The prophet Isaiah connects the discipline of fasting to the discipline of seeking justice:

> *Is not this the fast that I choose:*
> *to loose the bonds of injustice,*
> *to undo the thongs of the yoke,*
> *to let the oppressed go free,*
> *and to break every yoke?* (Isaiah 58:6)

In whatever way we choose to participate, the Church gives us forty days to prepare our hearts and lives for the great miracle of Easter. How will you fast before the feast?

How to Use This Book

This activity book follows the season of Lent from Ash Wednesday through Holy Week and Easter Sunday. It includes activities that explore the themes of Lent and includes Bible stories that are often part of our scripture reading during this season of spiritual cleansing and renewal.

Families

This book can be used by families at home as adults and children learn together about Lent. The pages are organized chronologically and can be used as family devotions exploring one page a day for the forty days of Lent. Two extra pages for Palm Sunday and Easter Sunday are included. Family devotions might be extended to included the following short prayer service

> *Gather as a family*
> *Light a candle*
> Leader: *Create in me a clean heart, O God*
> Response: *and renew a right spirit within me.*
> *Read the Bible verse from the activity page*
> *Explore the activity page together*
> *Close with one of the following prayers:*

Almighty God, you know that we often wander far away from your love: Pour out your mercy on us whenever we go astray, help us to turn away from our sinful desires, and bring us again into your loving embrace; through Jesus Christ our Lord, who lives and loves with you and the Holy Spirit, one God now and for ever. Amen.

– or –

God of mercy, when we roam
Call us back safely home. Amen.

– or –

Dear God, be good to me; the sea is so wide and my boat is so small. Amen.

Christian Educators

Christian educators will also find this book useful in a parish setting for Church School classes and children's worship times. The pages can be added to Sunday Kid's Packs. The activities will help children be more aware of the significance of the Church Year and themes of Lent. The pages also tell the biblical stories about the ministry of Jesus.

Using this book with non-readers

Toddlers and preschool children respond to the world around them with their senses. They are aware of what they see, hear, touch, and smell even before they have names for things and words to describe them. They can happily engage with the activity pages on their own with crayons or markers. Then they can engage at a deeper level when an adult sits down and reads the pages to them.

Using this book with readers

Early elementary children will enjoy reading and completing the pages on their own. However, don't miss the opportunity of learning from your children by engaging them in conversation about what they discover. Invite them to tell you what captures their attention, what they are curious about, or what these activities tell them about God. Children have valuable theological insights and by listening to them adults can be inspired.

Ash Wednesday

Ash Wednesday is the beginning of Lent. On this day we mark our foreheads with ashes. This reminds us that God created human beings out of the dust of the earth and that one day we will return to dust.

Mark a cross on each person's forehead.

"Remember that you are dust, and to dust you shall return."
(Book of Common Prayer p.265)

Keeping a Holy Lent

To _____ means to turn around. During _____ we look at our lives to see if we are going in the right direction. We _____ to God to help us. We _____ the bible to help us know the way. We _____ to make us more mindful of what we truly need. We reach out to others who need our _____.

Lent   help   fast   repent   pray   study

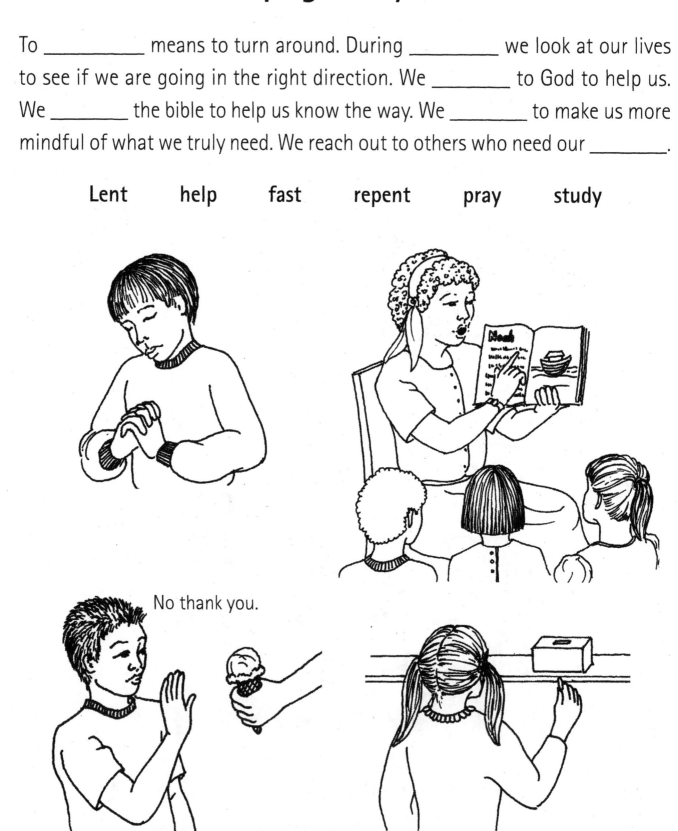

No thank you.

Repent, for the Kingdom of God had come near. Matthew 3:2

Church Year Calendar

Lent is the season leading up to Easter. It lasts for forty days, beginning on Ash Wednesday and continuing through Hold Saturday. Sundays in Lent are not counted as part of the forty days, because Sundays are always feast days.

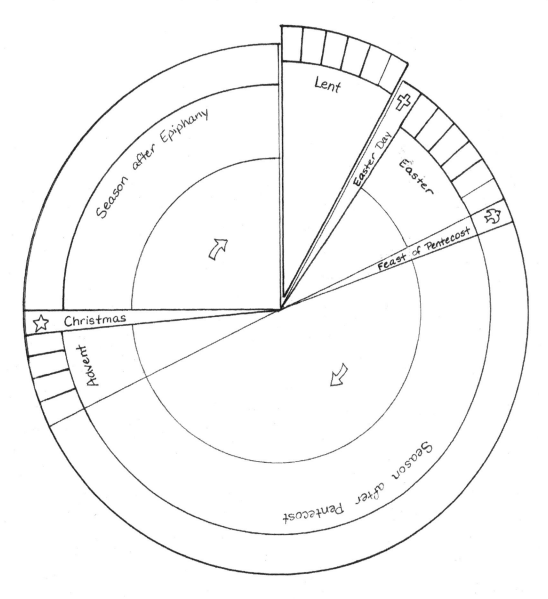

Each Church season has a different color. Color the seasons according to the key:

Lent – Purple

Easter – Gold

Feast of Pentecost – Red

Season after Pentecost – Green

Advent – Blue or Purple

Christmas – Gold

Season after Epiphany – Green

For everything there is a season, and a time for every matter under heaven. Ecclesiastes 3:1

The Temptation of Jesus

Jesus wanders in the desert for 40 days and is faced with many temptations. Help Jesus find his way through the desert and away from temptation.

Jesus was in the wilderness forty days, tempted by Satan; and he was with the wild beasts; and the angels waited on him. Mark 1:13

A Sacred Journey

Lent is a forty day journey for us. Connect the dots to discover another important forty day event from the bible.

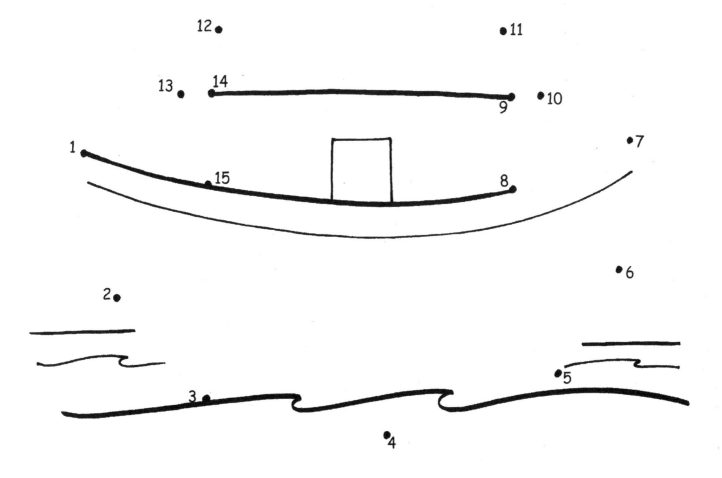

God said to Noah, "Bring two of every kind of living thing, male and female, into the ark with you." Genesis 6:19

Colors of Lent

In Lent we try to keep the Church simple, using somber colors or no color at all. Some Church's use deep purple. Some use a Lenten Array, which is plain cloth. What color does your parish use in Lent?

Write the names under the objects and color them in the Lenten color used in your church.

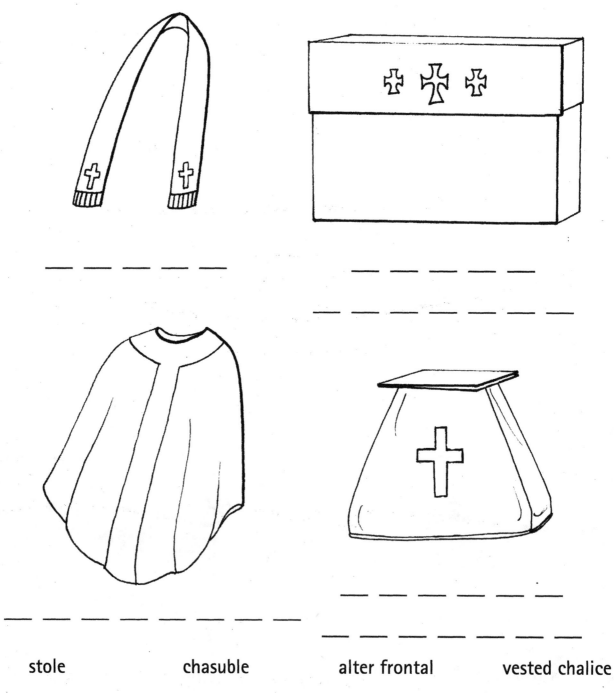

| stole | chasuble | alter frontal | vested chalice |

The Lord is in his holy temple; let all the earth keep silence before him. Habakkuk 2:20

Prayers of Praise

Lent is a time to practice prayer. Draw or write a prayer praising God.

Let the peoples praise you, O God; let all the peoples praise you. Psalm 67:3

Temptation Word Search

Jesus was tempted by Satan in the wilderness. He ate nothing for forty days and forty nights, and he was very hungry. First the devil tempted him to turn stones into bread, so he could eat. Next the devil tempted Jesus to throw himself off the temple tower and let the angels catch him. Finally the devil tried to get Jesus to worship him by offering the kingdoms of the world. But Jesus said, "No!" Matthew 4:1-11

```
Y Q J S P N M P R Q
B Q O L I O T S E T
D D B E D I H A S T
I B F G O T U F S O
E S N N A N X T G
G I T A F T G R O R
K B T O V P E A W I
M A S Y N M R X E X
S F D E S E R T R P
B R E A D T S W P Q
```

See if you can find these words.

tempation   tower
desert   hunger
satan   angels
bread   test
stones   kingdom

The Sign of the Cross

The cross is a symbol that reminds us not only that Jesus died, but more importantly that he rose from the dead. When we make the sign of the cross, we are remembering our baptisms and that we will die one day but that we will also rise to new life with Jesus.

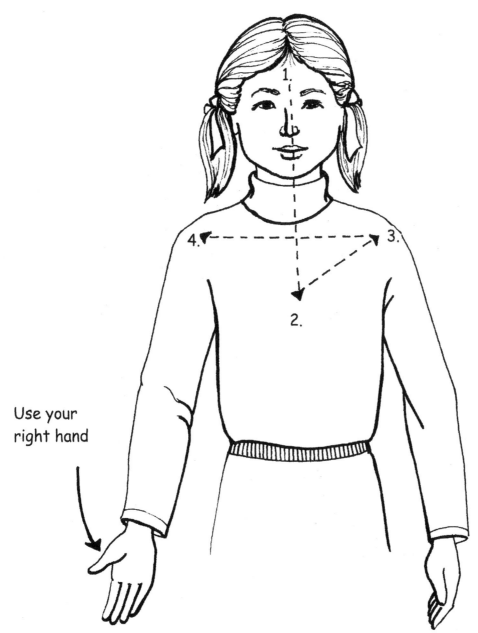

Use your right hand

Practice making the sign of the cross

As many of your as were baptized into Christ have clothed yourselves with Christ. Galatians 3:27

The Widow's Mite

Once Jesus watched people giving money to the temple. Many rich people gave a lot. One poor woman, a widow, put in two pennies. Jesus said that she gave more. The rich people gave to God from what they had left over. But the poor woman gave all that she had. Mark 12:41-44

The word "mite" means a very small amount. During Lent, many people use a mite box to collect money for those in need. Draw coins in the girl's hand which she can put in her mite box.

Nicodemus

Nicodemus was a teacher in Israel. He came to visit Jesus at night. Jesus told him something very important. (John 3:1-10)

Color in the letters with a cross on them to see what Jesus told Nicodemus.

Prayers of Confession

Lent is a time to practice prayer. Draw or write a prayer telling God you are sorry.

In you, O Lord, have I taken refuge; let me never be put to shame; deliver me in your righteousness. Psalm 31:1

Lent Word Search

```
S B N A R I T U P J
S A H O W H F D R G
N S C J O H M V A B
W F O R T Y D A Y S
O C N R I I O E E Z
R S J U C F V G R C
C S E H S A I T F A
U F A S T K N C N O
W E K O B E H P E Y
M S G D L M F S K F
```

See if you can find these lenten words in the puzzle

Lent	fast	crown
prayer	cross	sacrifice
ashes	forty days	thorns

Bear fruit worthy of repentance. Matthew 3:8

Promises

Lent is a time to remember God's promises. God promised Sarah and Abraham a large family with many generations. Sarah and Abraham are our ancestors!

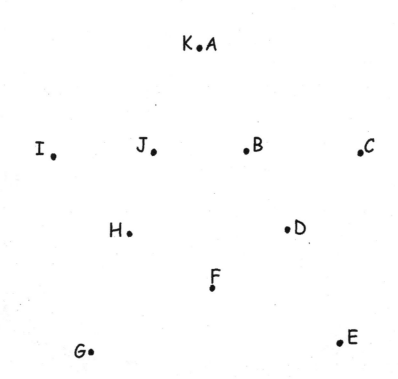

God told Abraham he would have more descendants than all of these. (Genesis 15:5) Connect the dots to discover what, and then add more to the picture.

Loaves and Fishes

Once Jesus fed a hungry crowd with only five loaves of _____ and _____ fish. After everyone ate, the people filled _____ baskets with the leftovers. Luke 9:10-17

twelve   **bread**   **two**

Draw more fish and bread pieces to keep the baskets filled.

Sign of the Covenant

When Noah and the Ark reached dry land after the flood, God made a covenan with Noah and the animals. A covenant is a special promise. God promised neve again would a flood destroy the earth. Color the hidden picture to find the symbo of God's promise to Noah.

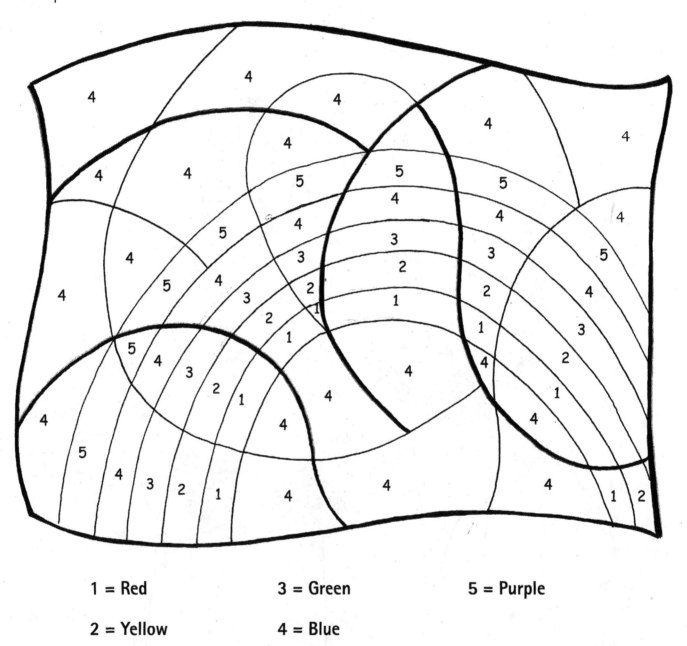

1 = Red	3 = Green	5 = Purple
2 = Yellow	4 = Blue	

God said to Noah, "This is a sign of the covenant that I make between me and you and every living creature." Genesis 9:12

Jesus Meets A Woman at the Well

Once while visiting Samaria, Jesus met a woman at a well. He told her that he could give her living water that would bring her new life. She believed in him. She ran to tell her friends and she brought them to meet Jesus.

John 4:5-42

Number the pictures in the right order.

Prayers of Thanksgiving

Lent is a time to practice prayer. Draw or write a prayer thanking God. Decorate the frame.

Put your trust in God; for I will yet give thanks to him, who is the help of my countenance, and my God. Psalm 43:6

What's Different About Lent?

During Lent we dress down the church. We make our worship space simple to symbolize this penitential season. Can you find five differences between these two pictures? Circle them.

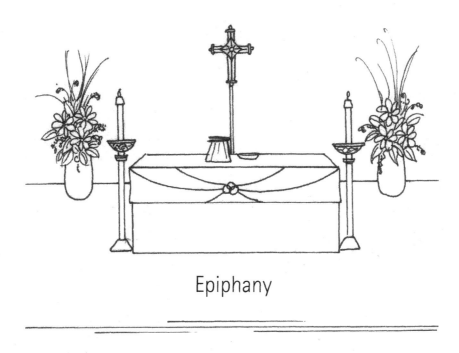

Epiphany

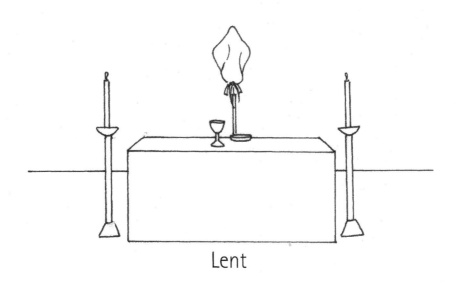

Lent

Ascribe to the Lord the glory due his Name; worship the Lord in the beauty of holiness. Psalm 29:2

Hidden Treasure

Find 12 hidden coins in this picture that can be given away.
Do you have any hidden treasure that could be given away?

For where your treasure is there your heart will be also. Matthew 6:21

I'm Sorry

Lent is a time to practice saying, "I'm sorry."

- Think about a choice you made that hurt someone.
- Tell God you are sorry.
- Draw a picture of yourself telling the person you hurt that you are sorry.

- Tell the person you are sorry. You can use words, or show them this picture, or write them a note.
- Read a story about a boy who was sorry in Luke 15:11-32

The Journey of Jesus

Trace a path to all the places Jesus traveled.

- Jesus grew up in Nazareth
- He turned water to wine in Cana
- He lived and taught in Capernaum
- He walked on water near Bethsaida
- He visited the people in Caesarea Philippi
- He healed a little girl near Tyre and Sidon
- He taught on the shore of the Sea of Galilee
- He healed a blind man in Jericho
- He raised Lazarus from the dead in Bethany
- He ate the Passover meal with his friends in Jerusalem

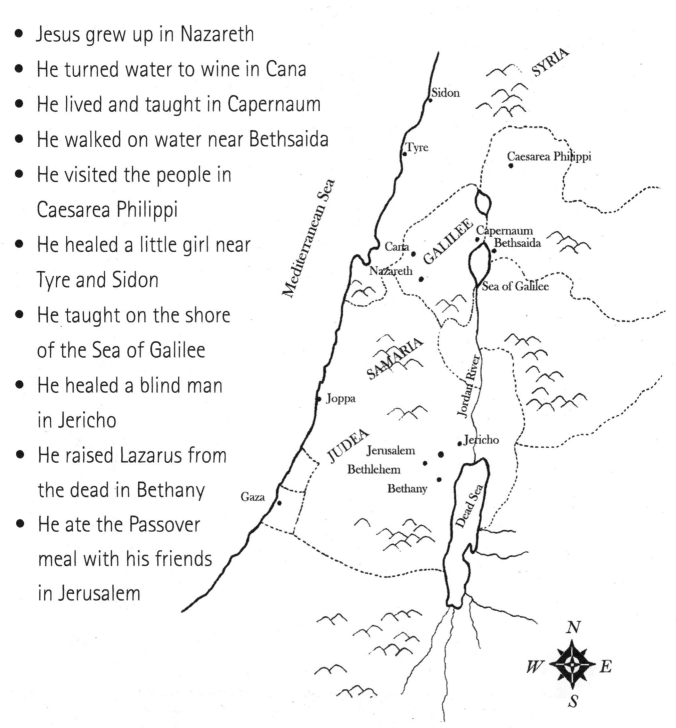

Then Jesus went about all the cities and villages, teaching in their synagogues, and proclaiming the good news of the kingdom, and curing every disease and every sickness. Matthew 9:35

Jesus Heals a Man Born Blind

Once Jesus met a young man who was born blind. He made some mud and put it on the man's eyes. he told the man to go and wash in the pool of Siloam. The man went and washed and he was able to see. he told everyone he met how Jesus had healed him.

John 9:1-41

Number the pictures in the right order.

Prayers of Intersession

Lent is a time to practice prayer. Draw or write a prayer asking God to help others.

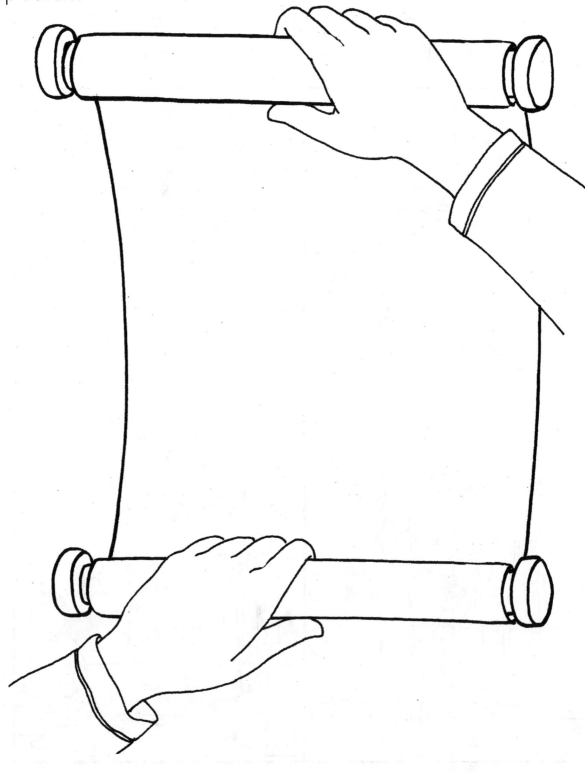

Answer me when I call, O God, defender of my cause. Psalm 4:1

Symbols of Sacrifice

Jesus gave up his life for us. He made a great sacrifice. To sacrifice means to give up something you love, because you love something else even more.

 The Crown of thorns reminds us that Jesus was a king who suffered.

 The Heart reminds us that Jesus' sacrifice was a gift of love.

 The Cross reminds us that Jesus gave his life for us.

 The Palm branch reminds us that Jesus' journey to the cross was one of hope.

Complete the pattern:

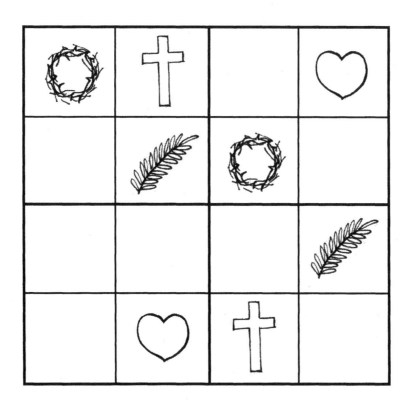

For God so loved the World that he gave his only Son. John 3:16

Wants and Needs

Things we want are different than things we need. Lent is a good time to think about what we really need. Look at the pictures below. Underline the things you want. Circle the things you need.

Draw a picture of the most important thing that you need.

Jesus told his friends not to worry about what to eat or drink or wear. "God knows what you need." Matthew 6:25-33

An Important Number

40 is an important number in the Bible and is used in many stories.

Moses

Fasted in the desert for 40 days.
(Matthew 4:2)

Mary

Wondered in the wilderness for 40 years.
(Deuteronomy 29:2–9)

Noah

Carried Jesus in her womb for 40 weeks.
(Luke 1:26–31)

Jesus

Traveled safely in the ark while it rained for
40 days. (Genesis 7:11–17)

Match each person with the correct story.

Count Your Blessings

Walk through your house and count how many of each of the pictured items you have.

_____

_____

_____

_____

_____

_____

Which of these could you share with someone who has less?

For I was hungry, and you gave me food. Matthew 25:35

Jesus Raises Lazarus From the Dead

Jesus heard that his friend Lazarus was sick. But by the time Jesus got to his house, his friend had died and was buried. Mary, the sister of Lazarus, asked Jesus for help. Jesus told them to remove the stone that covered the tomb. He called to his friend, "Lazarus, come out!" Jesus raised Lazarus to life.

John 11:1-44

Number the pictures in the right order.

Prayers of Petition

Lent is a time to practice prayer. Draw or write a prayer asking God to help you.

The Lord has heard my supplication; the Lord accepts my prayer. Psalm 6:9

New Life

Lent is a time to prepare for new life. Jesus said, "Unless a seed falls into the earth and dies, it remains just a seed." John 12:24

Color the picture to discover what seeds can become.

1 = Green   3 = Pink   5 = Yellow   2 = Blue

The Garden

Jesus and his disciples went to a _____ called Gethsemane to pray.
Jesus was very _____. He _____ to God. Matthew 26:36-40

sad   garden   prayed

Write or draw your prayer for the season of Lent.

When is Holy Week?

Fill in the month and dates. Outline Holy Week in red. Circle Easter Sunday in gold. Decorate your calendar.

The Month of _____

Sunday	Monday	Tuesday	Wednesday	Thursday	Friday	Saturday
Palm Sunday	Monday in Holy Week	Tuesday in Holy Week	Wednesday in Holy Week	Maundy Thursday	Good Friday	Holy Saturday
Easter Sunday	Monday in Easter Week	Tuesday in Easter Week	Wednesday in Easter Week	Thursday in Easter Week	Friday in Easter Week	Saturday in Easter Week

Why is one day more important than another, when all the daylight in the year is from the sun? By the Lord's wisdom they were distinguished, and he appointed the different seasons and festivals. Some days he exalted and hallowed, and some he made ordinary days. Ecclesiasticus (Sirach) 33:7-9

Palm Sunday

When Jesus and his disciples came near _____, he sent two disciples into the village ahead of them, where they found a donkey tied just as Jesus had said they would. They brought him the _____ and Jesus sat on it as he rode into Jerusalem. A very large _____ gathered. The people spread cloaks and _____ branches on the road ahead of him shouting, "Hosanna to the Son of David! Blessed is the one who comes in the name of the Lord! _____ in the highest heaven!"

Matthew 21:1-11

crowd   Jerusalem   Hosanna   palm   donkey

Help Jesus find a path through the crowd to reach Jerusalem. Draw palms and cloaks along the path.

Monday in Holy Week
Jesus Cleanses the Temple

Jesus taught in the _____, and many came to hear him. When he saw many people buying and selling in the temple grounds, he became angry. He drove them out saying, "Remember it is written, My house shall be called a house of _____ but you are making it a den of _____." Then he _____ all who came to him. Matthew 21:13

robbers   temple   healed   prayer

Draw someone who Jesus is healing.

Tuesday in Holy Week
The Greatest Commandment

A lawyer asked Jesus, "Teacher, which commandment is the greatest?" Jesus answered, "You shall _____ the Lord your God with all your heart, and with all your soul, and with all your mind. And you shall _____ your neighbor as yourself."

Matthew 22:36-38

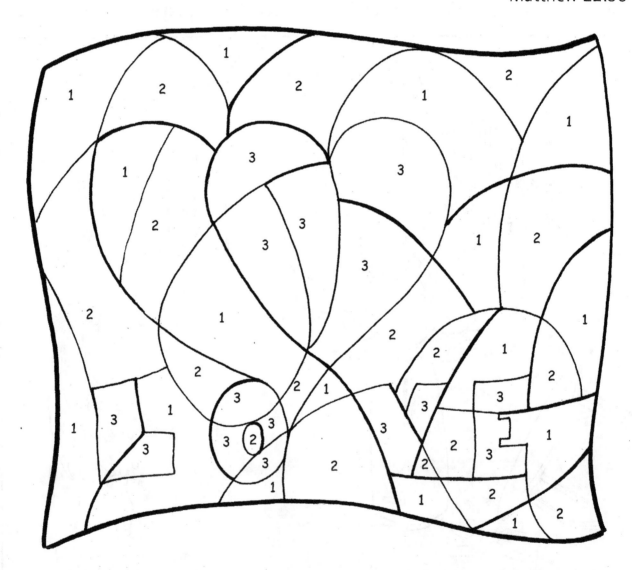

Color the hidden picture to discover the greatest commandment.

1 – Blue　　　　**2 – Green**　　　　**3 – Red**

Wednesday in Holy Week
A Woman Anoints Jesus

Jesus said, "Truly I tell you, wherever the good news is proclaimed in the whole world, what she has done will be told in remembrance of her."
Mark 14:9

Color the picture.

Maunday Thursday

On the night before he died, Jesus ate a special meal with his friends.
Follow the dot-to-dot to see what food and drink he shared with them.

Jesus said, "This is my body which is given for you. Do this in
remembrance of me." Luke 22:19

Good Friday

Follow the way of the cross.

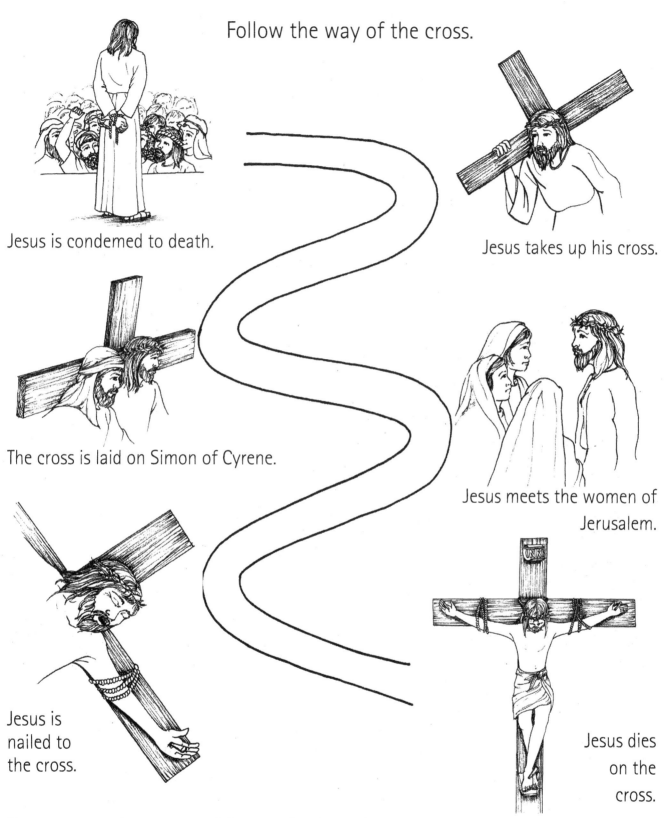

Jesus is condemed to death.

Jesus takes up his cross.

The cross is laid on Simon of Cyrene.

Jesus meets the women of Jerusalem.

Jesus is nailed to the cross.

Jesus dies on the cross.

If any want to become my followers, let them deny themselves and take up their cross and follow me. Mark 8:34

Holy Saturday

Joseph of Arimathea took the body of Jesus and wrapped it in a clean linen cloth and laid it in his own new tomb, which had been hewn in the rock. He then rolled a stone to the door of the tomb and went away. Matthew 27:59-60

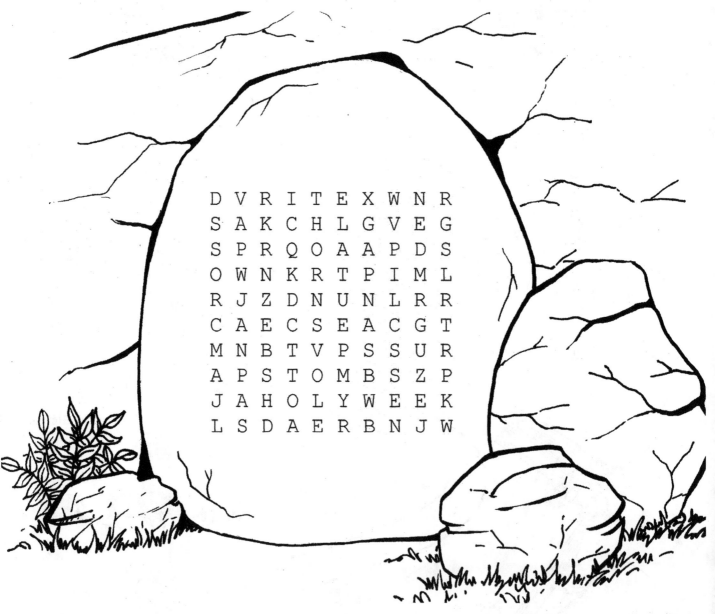

```
D V R I T E X W N R
S A K C H L G V E G
S P R Q O A A P D S
O W N K R T P I M L
R J Z D N U N L R R
C A E C S E A C G T
M N B T V P S S U R
A P S T O M B S Z P
J A H O L Y W E E K
L S D A E R B N J W
```

See if you can find these holy week words in the puzzle.

holy week	thorns	garden
cup	cross	palms
bread	darkness	tomb
trial	last supper	

Mary at the Tomb

Early Easter morning, Mary Magdalene went to visit Jesus' tomb. An angel met her and told her Jesus had risen! Matthew 28:5

Find these hidden pictures.

The Church Year

The Church year really consists of two great feasts: Easter Day, the date of which is movable, and Christmas Day which is always December 25. Easter Day is always the first Sunday after the full moon that falls on or after March 21. Based on these two feasts, the Church Year is divided into seasons: Advent, Christmas, Epiphany, Lent, Easter, and Pentecost.

Advent is the beginning of the Church year. "Advent" means "the coming," and the first Sunday of Advent is four Sundays before Christmas. During Advent we wait for the birth of Christ and we anticipate Christ's second coming. The color for Advent is usually purple (for royalty) or blue (for peace). We celebrate Christmas, or the Feast of the Nativity, for twelve days, from December 25 to January 6. The color for Christmas is white or gold. January 6 is the Feast of the Epiphany, when we celebrate the visit of the Magi to the Christ child. The color for the Feast of Epiphany is white, but the Sundays following Epiphany are green. The Epiphany season runs from January 6 to Ash Wednesday and varies in length from six to nine weeks.

Ash Wednesday is the beginning of Lent. Lent is the forty days before Easter and is a time of fasting and preparation for the great celebration of Easter. The forty days represents the time Jesus spent fasting in the wilderness at the beginning of his ministry. The five Sundays in Lent are not considered fast days and are not counted in the forty. The color for Lent is usually purple (royalty and penitence), but some churches use vestments in a natural linen with no color (for simplicity). Lent ends with Holy Week: Palm Sunday, Maundy Thursday, Good Friday, and Holy Saturday. The color for Holy Week is red.

The Easter Season begins with the Great Vigil of Easter on Easter Eve followed by Easter Day, or the Sunday of the Resurrection. We celebrate Easter for fifty days, called The Great Fifty Days, until the Feast of Pentecost. On the fortieth day of Easter we celebrate Ascension Day, when the resurrected Christ ascended into Heaven. The color of Easter is white or gold.

The Feast of Pentecost is the last day of the Easter Season. We celebrate the coming of the Holy Spirit and the beginning of the Church. The color for the Feast of Pentecost is red (for fire and the Holy Spirit). The Sundays after Pentecost until Advent are called the Season after Pentecost. The color for this season is green (for growing and new life).

Holy Week and the Triduum

Holy Week begins with Palm Sunday. With the reading of the story of Jesus' triumphal entry into Jerusalem, we begin a week devoted to remembering the last days of Jesus' life on earth. Monday, Tuesday, and Wednesday of Holy Week are days of special devotion leading us to the Triduum, the three great holy days of Maundy Thursday, Good Friday, and the Great Vigil of Easter. On Maundy Thursday we remember when Jesus gathered with his friends for the last supper. He washed their feet, offered them bread and the cup and told them, "I give you a new commandment, that you love one another as I have loved you." The Latin for "new commandment" is *mandatum novum*, so this is where we get the name Maundy Thursday. On Good Friday we remember the death of Jesus on the cross. Although this is a very sad day for all who love Jesus, we call it good because of the ultimate good that triumphs over evil in the death and resurrection of Christ. Without death, there is no resurrection. On Holy Saturday we live into that death and the emptiness. Then, as evening falls, we celebrate the Great Vigil of Easter. We kindle a new fire, light the Paschal candle for the first time, tell the ancient stories of our tradition, and celebrate the first Eucharist of Easter.

The Disciplines of Lent

The Book of Common Prayer invites us to the observance of a Holy Lent. The traditional disciplines of Lent include prayer, study, fasting, and outreach. Rather than simply thinking of what we can "give up" for Lent, we can consider these traditional areas and think of how we can engage them in new ways.

- Prayer: Perhaps your household could take on a family prayer discipline for Lent, such as the one described in "How to Use This Book" on p. [TK]. You could also look for opportunities to include prayer in your household life, such as saying grace before meals or sharing bedtime prayers as a family.

- Study: Reading Bible stories together is a great way for all family members to become more familiar with Holy Scripture. Younger children will enjoy Bible picture books. Older youth can be introduced to stories in the family Bible or their own Bibles. Try some the books recommended in the resource section below.

- Fasting: To fast does not always mean to go completely without food. While it can mean total abstinence for a certain amount of time, it can also mean to eat less or more simply. In some traditions, eating only one meal a day after sundown is considered fasting. In some cases, fasting means eating only simple foods, like bread and water, during the day. Choose one night a week to eat more simply during Lent.

- Outreach: Why not take on a household project to support an outreach ministry during Lent? As a family you could collect food for a local food bank or volunteer at a meal center. You could collect the money you would normally spend on treats and choose to donate it to mission work. Several suggestions are listed in the resource section below.

Resources

Devotions and activities

The Anglican Family Prayer Book, Anne E. Kitch, Morehouse, 2004.
    Prayers and family devotions for the church year.

Easter Garden Book, C. E. Visminas, Morehouse, 2001.
    An activity book to create the garden of Jesus' burial.

Easter Mural Book, C. E. Visminas, Morehouse, 2001.
    A beautiful mural to decorate.

Forty Days and Forty Nights: A Lenten Ark Moving toward Easter, Peter Mazar, Judy Jarrett, ill., Liturgical Training Publications, 1995.
    A 3-D Lenten calendar shaped like Noah's ark with doors to open for each of the forty days.

A Path to Easter, Helen Barron, Candle Press, 2007.
    Family devotions for Lent.

Through the Cross, Helen Barron, Candle Press, 2007.
    Family activities for Holy Week.

Year of Grace Poster Calendar, art by Kathy Ann Sullivan, Liturgical Training Publications.
    A beautifully illustrated poster of the Church Year. A new one is designed each year.

Books

At Jerusalem's Gate: Poems of Easter, Nikki Grimes and David Framptom, ills., Eerdmans, 2005.

Bible Stories for the Forty Days, Melissa Musick Nussbaum and Judy Jarrett, ills., Liturgical Training Publications, 1998.

The Easter Story, Brian Wildsmith, Eerdmans, 2000.

Love One Another: The Last Days of Jesus, Lauren Thompson and Elizabeth Uyehara, ill., Scholastic, 2000.

The Story of the Cross: The Stations of the Cross for Children, Mary Joslin, Loyola Press, 2002.

Outreach Ideas

Episcopal Relief and Development www.er-d.org
    Has great resources for families and children, including mite boxes and a *Gifts for Life Catalogue*, that help children and families worldwide.

Heifer Project International www.heifer.org
    Provides training and animals gifts for children and families around the world that help them become self-reliant. Has mite boxes and calendars for children to use as devotions.

The One Campaign www.one.org
    Works to eradicate extreme poverty. Has a wealth of ideas, projects and donation possibilities. Works in conjunction with the Millennium Development goals (MDGs).

CPSIA information can be obtained
at www.ICGtesting.com
Printed in the USA
JSHW022216151022
31677JS00001B/1